Homefires

War through the eyes of a military wife

Sherry Hines

www.justawife.net

P.O. Box 353, Ft Campbell, KY 42223

Design of cover by John Slinger

Inside specifications by Michael and Diane at Presto Services, Inc.

Editing done by Billy Metz, Mary Jo Hendrix, Betsy Murray, Jenn Generoso

Library of Congress
Homefires
1. Self- publishing 2. Self- publishing
I. Title
Library of Congress Control Number 2004094212
ISBN 0-9758651-0-2
This is the revised edition of Homefires. This is the second print of the revised Homefires.

Published by Just A Wife

For Those Left Behind

This book is dedicated to those left behind. Never forget that you are doing your part for your country. Don't think that because your job is behind the scenes, it is any less vital.

www.saluteheroes.org
All of the charities are wonderful, but this one is near and dear to my heart. These are soldiers helping soldiers. I am so proud of them. After everything they have been through, they have the courage to put their self out there in the public eye to help others. I hope all of you do whatever you can for this organization.

I want to thank God for loving me with all my many, many faults. Just as I am. I would like to thank my husband and son for being who you are. Mom, Billi, Jenn, and Betsy for your patience and editing. Mell and David for helping make books and for your encouragement. Michael and Diane without whom this wouldn't have happened. Brent for enlisting volunteers. John a stranger who volunteered his time and knowledge. Carol for opening up her heart and store to me. Candi for the title. If I didn't mention you by name you are not any less appreciated. Thank you all for believing in why I am doing this, the book, and me.

www.saluteheroes.org

Introduction

I'm no one special. I am just an average military wife and stay-at-home mother. I guess it makes me sound full of myself thinking anyone cares what I have to say, but it's not like that. My husband is in combat arms; that is why I don't mention women. This would apply to the husbands left behind. I just don't know any of them. On this edition I took some things out and added new ones, because I don't want anything to distract from the purpose of the book. This is about the families not political.

For those not in the military, I don't represent anyone but myself. I don't speak for all military wives. I can only express what my friends and I have gone through. That being said, I want others to see what we go through, because the news doesn't give a clue as to what we feel. Letting others see the things I've written is a little like standing outside naked. Not that I've stood outside naked, I would hate to scare the neighbors. I just thought it was important to do this.

For military wives, I would like them to know they are not the only ones to have felt those feelings or to have had those moments. Sometimes we are too concerned about keeping it together and being everything to everyone. We forget we are just people trying to get through a difficult time. You don't have to be everything to everyone. If you try to be, you will burn out.

I am a strong capable woman who has moments of doubt, fear, uncertainty, anger and sadness. It doesn't make me any less strong, it makes me human. I don't walk around weighed down by things. I just have moments, and if you don't then you should be the one writing a book. Please don't forget to send me one. I would love to read it. I try to look on the positive side and provide a full, happy life for my son. Some of the things I say sound extreme, but if I am sitting down to write, they are extreme. This is my release and keeps me from going crazy.

I hope that someone reads at least one thing I write and feels better knowing they are not alone. If after reading this you think I am crazy, well maybe I am. My heart belongs to a military man, and if that isn't crazy I don't know what is.

SHERRY HINES

*　*　*　*　*　*　*

Before my husband left for Kuwait, his A-bag was packed and we were waiting for the word to go. The word to go came several times. It became an almost daily event. We said goodbye and then he came home. The Army is big on doing things over and over until they get it right, I guess they thought they should extend this to the families. The day finally did come and it made me grateful for everyday he didn't go.

*　*　*　*　*　*　*

Goodbye

They stand by the truck knowing they have put this off as long as possible. He says he has to go now. She suddenly can't hold back the tears. He looks down, holding her face in his hands. Then with a slight smile he wipes away her tears. He tells her, " I love you and we will get through just like we always have." She tells him, " I love you. May God's speed bring you home to me."

The tender kiss so achingly sweet leaves her staring after him. No matter how many times she sees him in uniform her heart still fills with pride.

She knows she has no choice. She has to get in the truck and drive away. She lets out a deep breath; her life has now changed. She knows he is already focused on the mission ahead, it's the only way he can do what he does. All she can do now is turn it over to God and accept it is all out of her control.

*   *   *   *   *   *   *

I was glued to the news like a lot of the others, but only when my son was asleep or at school. It took protesters to get me away from it. It made me so mad to see them that I had to turn off the TV. It also got me out of the house and involved in the support rallies. There is no way to describe what it feels like to be at a rally. At the very least, it gave me something I could feel like I was doing, instead of just waiting.

*   *   *   *   *   *   *

Support Rally

I pull up and get my sign from the trunk. I am amazed how many people are here. I guess everyone else is sick of the protesters and want a chance to show our guys that this is not how America feels. I realize that our guys are fighting for their right to protest, but the things they say make me mad enough to spit. What is wrong with these people? Are they blind? Do they not see what our guys are doing?

Looking up, down and across the street, it is lined with supporters holding signs. People driving out of their way, so they can come to honk their horns to show support for the guys. I was blown away when I started seeing local news crews, but when I saw CNN I realized I was involved in something that could make a difference. Everyone is there, from children, to mothers, to wives, to bikers. There are people there that don't even have anyone in the military; they just want to show support for the troops. The speakers really get everyone pumped up. Patriotism radiates from the crowd.

Everyone is wearing various red, white, and blues. Some posters are simple and to the point. While others are more elaborate. The one I'll never forget is this little boy holding a sign almost as big as he was. He had blue eyes to match the ones in the picture on his sign. Above it read " My Daddy Is A Hero". It brought tears to my eyes. For military families this is really what it is all about. They are heroes and we won't let anyone say differently.

Your Country

What happened to, “Ask not what your country can do for you—ask what you can do for your country?” [1] People want freedom and what they deem their rights, however they don’t want to do anything to ensure they keep them. Rights and freedoms are balanced with responsibility and duty. They want their rights as long as they’re not asked to sacrifice to have them. At what point did we go from being a country full of resourceful, inventive, God-fearing pioneers to a country where there are too many anti-Christian, lazy slackers who have their hand out at every turn? I believe our founding fathers meant for us to be responsible for ourselves, like adults should be. I’m not saying people don’t deserve help when they fall on hard times, but it should be reserved for people who really do need it. It shouldn’t be expected it is their due that the government take care of them. Can you imagine today’s average American, myself included, picking up and heading out west with nothing but a wagon. We need to look back to where we came from and decide where we want this country to go.

We have the ability to achieve greatness. If Americans could unite with a common goal of getting the country back to what it was meant to be, there would be no limit to what we could achieve. I think we can have diversity in a united goal to better our country. We all want the same thing: to leave a better world for our children.

[1] quoted John F. Kennedy, Inaugural Address, 1961

*   *   *   *   *   *   *

On March 23, 2003, Hasan K. Akbar allegedly rolled grenades into tents and shot 2 soldiers as they rushed out. He was charged with 17 counts of attempted murder and aggravated arson. I hope they put him under the prison. Bad, bad man.

*   *   *   *   *   *   *

She gets up and stumbles in the kitchen, stopping to turn on the news. She always tries to catch up on it before the kids get up. While getting the coffee going, she makes a mental to do list for the day. She suddenly stops dead still. "What did they say?" she asks out loud. Grabbing the remote she turns up the volume. Already soldiers are dying, and they haven't left Kuwait yet.

She wonders, " How did the enemy get in that camp?"

"Oh dear God it was one of our own." Numb, she sits on the couch. Her mind races, "I knew to worry about the enemy. I knew there would be friendly fire accidents. Who would think I would need to fear one of our own? Why? "

"So many whys. Are the soldiers married? Do they have kids? Oh no, what camp is it? Thank God, it's not my husbands. I hate to be selfish, but he will always come first."

"A new worry. 'Cause there is just not enough of those to go around. What about the guy in the cot next to my husband? I know them, but I'm sure Akbar's fellow soldiers thought they knew him. Does this mean they have people planted in our army or is this guy just a nut?"

For me it has truly begun.

*　　*　　*　　*　　*　　*　　*

Mail was a real issue. It took so long to get the first letter; there was no word at all. It was scary and frustrating. We all know it was the way things had to be at the time, but knowing and living with it are very different.

Even once the mail got going, it took a long time to get letters back and forth. Once they could call, they still couldn't call often because it was very expensive. The first phone call I got was unexpected at 3:00 am. It was free but timed either 3 or 5 minutes. By the time I woke up and had my head together it was over. I'm not complaining, because I was very grateful for the time I had to talk. Hearing his voice was priceless.

*　　*　　*　　*　　*　　*　　*

Mail Call

First thing in the morning, my son runs to the mailbox in his footie pajamas. " Son, the mail doesn't run until late afternoon." I say to thin air as he runs down the drive.

He comes home from school, jumps out of the car again running to the mailbox. He walks away sad, no letter from Daddy. "Honey, the mail hasn't run yet."

He gets up from his nap. " Momma, is the mail here yet?" " Yes Baby, go check it." He hits the door at a dead run. As the screen door slams into the rail, I decide I'd better follow.

He comes to me with a smile from ear to ear. Waving his letter in the air, and wanting it read for him. I open the envelope while he waits for the words he longs to hear. I tell him, " Daddy loves you and misses you so much. He's proud of you and can't wait to see you again." He skips to his room, so happy to hear from his daddy.

I let out a sigh, and fold up the bill to put with the others. I'm sure God will forgive me for these little white lies. It means so much to him and I know my husband will write as soon as he can. Hopefully, after the war has ended the mail will start running. Until then I'll pray my son doesn't learn to read before his daddy comes home.

Uncertainty

Am I selfish to have the thoughts I have? Is it wrong or human nature? When a soldier is lost, are you wrong to feel relief it's not your branch of service, same town, same unit or simply not yours?

Or is it human nature to feel the relief after holding your breath? This bothered me for quite some time. My heart goes out to the family of a lost soldier. I can only imagine their pain, and pray I never know it.

I finally asked a friend whose husband was in the Gulf War. She explained that most people feel the same thing, and that the relief I feel doesn't diminish the sympathy I feel for those who lost someone. I guess in the end we can't control our feelings and just have to accept that one emotion doesn't take away from the other. We can pray for peace, for those grieving and continued safety of our own soldier. We cannot however berate ourselves for things beyond our control.

The Knock

The mother hears the knock on the door, wondering who could it be this late. Soldiers? Why would soldiers be at my door? My son? No, not my son, there must be a mistake. I just heard from him. In her mind she sees flashes of memories: a toddler taking his first steps, a small boy starting kindergarten, his dirty ball uniform, his first girlfriend, teaching him to drive, in his cap and gown at graduation. Watching the boy leave for basic, knowing he will come back a man. But the one that stays, is the last one she has.

The wife hears the knock at the door. She knew about the accident, but didn't want to believe it could be him. Even now as she hears it, it couldn't be him. If she doesn't answer it, will that make it not true? In her mind she sees flashes of memories: the day they met, their first kiss, seeing him so young and happy, on one knee asking for her hand, their wedding day with him waiting at the end of the aisle. The day her son was born, looking as though he is the only man to father a child, pride shining in his eyes. But the one that stays, is the last one she has.

The son hears the knock on the door. He wonders who is here. He gets up and walks in the room rubbing his sleepy eyes. Mommy, what's wrong? Why are there soldiers? Why are you crying? What do you mean Daddy isn't coming home? He promised. In his mind he sees flashes of memories: getting in bed with Mom and Dad, peddling his bike and looking back to see Daddy smiling, trying again and again until he could cast his pole just like Dad, Daddy putting him to bed with a kiss. But the one that stays, is the last one he has.

The soldier looks at his mom, hugs her, and says I love you. Watch out for my wife and son. He turns to his wife with a hug and kiss. I love you, Honey. Be strong and we will be together soon. He kneels to his son. I love you, Buddy. Be a good boy and help Momma. I promise I'll be home as soon as I can. As he walks away he prays. Lord, please take care of them. If I don't come home, let the love that I've given them be enough to give them the strength to go on.

Reality

Walking through the door caught up in the drama of my own life, I throw down the keys, and lay on the couch. Grabbing the remote and flipping through the news for information relating to my husband, I suddenly stop mesmerized by the sight of Marines lying on their stomachs firing their weapons behind mounds of sand. My heart goes out to their wives. In my mind I can see them straining to see if it is their husband. What if one of these guys was shot on the air? I can't imagine what the families are going through.

Just when you think you have it bad, something comes along to remind you of all the blessings you have been given. I am sure through this year I will look back on this, and think of those wives. I hope it is a tool I will use to keep things in perspective.

Midnight

I check the news before going to bed. My stomach knots up. There's an explosion in Baghdad. Now another. My mind races. Will they target Mosul where my husband is? He has a mission tonight. Where and what is he doing? They, whoever they are, hit three cities in one day killing a soldier in our unit. I flip through the channels to find more information. It's midnight, how long can I stay up watching news and still do everything tomorrow?

Losing a soldier in our unit must have affected me more than I thought. How will she face tomorrow? How will she tell her kids?

I check the news again, there's another explosion in Baghdad. Is my husband ok? Will I hear from him tomorrow? If not, how will I know why I did not? I say a quick prayer. Please God, keep my husband safe and everyone else. Lord, keep him safe, if not for him or me, for my son. He really needs his daddy.

It's 12:15, but I can't sleep, not knowing what is happening. Every soldier I see on the news is someone's husband, father, brother, or son. Are there any soldiers hurt? I try to stay away from the news, because if something happens you just can't walk away.

Will there be a knock on my door? If so would I have the strength to open it? Once you open it, you can't close it again. Now they are reporting two blasts. Which is it two or three? They report as it happens, sometimes it's just not accurate.

It's 12:30, I've got to go to bed or I'll be grumpy with my son tomorrow. He has enough on his four-year-old shoulders. I don't want him to ever doubt that I'm always here, always going to take care of him, and I have everything under control.

March, I just have to focus on March. He will come home and everything will be okay. My husband is a soldier; this is what he does. I am a wife; this is what I do. We both serve our country with love and pride.

*   *   *   *   *   *   *

Mid way through the deployment my mother-in-law was hit by a car and put in the ICU. Fortunately, my son was spending the night with family and I was able to go straight to her. I sent a Red Cross message to my husband. Red Cross told me it might take a day or two for him to get it due to blackouts. I knew they couldn't help it, but I didn't have a day or two. It was touch and go with her, so I called my Family Readiness Group (FRG) to get advice. Up the chain it went, and before I knew it I was on the phone with the Rear- detachment Captain. With their help I was speaking to my husband in a matter of hours. They were all amazing and so came through for me. It just reinforced how important FRG can be to all of us. My husband was sent home and we stayed at the hospital in shifts so there was someone to take care of my son. I hadn't seen my husband in five months and we were thrown in a very difficult situation. Thankfully we pulled together. At first I was really worried with everything going on that the stress would be too much for us. I think thirteen years of marriage and all the trials and tribulations that go with it helped us pull through it.

*   *   *   *   *   *   *

FRG

The women left behind. Some are strangers and some are close friends. All united in a bond of pride, love, worry and strength. When one stumbles there is always another to pick her up.

We stand by each other in emergencies, pregnancies, moves, problems with kids, worries over spouses, and everything in between. When we lose one of our own, we lean together so that we all stay standing. We share our tears, our fears, our laughter, and our joy.

We go to support rallies to show our pride in our husbands and country. We work tirelessly on various fundraisers, just so all of our soldiers have a package at Christmas.

There is a pride and strength in these women so rarely seen. I am so proud to be a part of them.

* * * * * * *

While my husband was home on emergency leave, we found out our landlord quit paying the mortgage and our house was going up for auction. I have no idea what they did with the rent I paid every month, but obviously it wasn't paying the mortgage. On top of everything else, I would now need to find a new home and move. My poor husband had to leave to go back to Iraq knowing he was leaving me to deal with it all on my own. It was very difficult for him, but such is life.

Since my son's school had started, I spent weekends in Memphis with my in-laws and weekdays at home. While at home, I would search all day until dark to find a new home. I was on a time crunch because of the auction.

Once I found a house, I had to move immediately. My mother came to help take care of my son. My dad and stepmother came and helped move the backyard, then took my son for a few days. Of course, it came a monsoon while I was moving boxes. As I carried dripping boxes in the house, I just kept telling myself it's not snowing and I'm not pregnant. That was as close to the bright side as I could come up with at the time. Guys from post came out to help my stepbrother and me move the big stuff. I'm sure after it was over I should have been proud of myself for getting through it. To be honest I just felt tired and drained. I can look back now and laugh at how crazy I was at the time. I remember falling asleep at a streetlight. When the horn of the car behind me woke me up, I realized that I couldn't go on without rest.

* * * * * * *

After Goodbye

Coming home from saying goodbye to her husband, she pauses by the door to take off her shoes. Then places them by her husband's boots, just as she does everyday. She thinks to herself I might as well put these away; he won't need them for a year at least. With a sigh, she reaches for them and hesitates. No, she will leave them. She wants to savor every reminder as long as she can. That night and several to follow, she sleeps in the shirt that still carries his scent. As she falls asleep, she wonders how long it will be until the reminders fade away.

Days turn into weeks and weeks turn into months. She finds herself packing the house to move all alone. She's getting use to doing things on her own. Moving box after box out the door to the new house she stumbles over his boots going out the door. They are still where he left them. She couldn't bring herself to move them. There is just something comforting about seeing them there.

After moving the last box out, she does a final walk through the empty house. Memories begin to flood her. Leaning against the doorway of her bedroom, she can almost see her husband reaching out to snuggle with her in the morning, trying to avoid starting the day. Checking her son's room he would be tucking their child into bed. Walking down the hallway she remembers him pulling her in the bathroom, with a house full of people, for a secret kiss. In the office packing his bags before leaving. Making her way into the kitchen, she gazes out the window. She smiles at the thought of her husband chasing their son in the backyard, while he grills their favorite meal. On her way to the door she can envision him on the couch. So tired from work he fell asleep with the dinner plate in his lap.

She bends down as she walks through the door, finally taking his boots with her. As she locks the door she prays. " Lord, don't let this be the last of my memories. Bring him home so we will have many years to make new ones."

*   *   *   *   *   *   *

Do you ever wonder if there is a woman in Iraq like us? Is she sitting in her living room wishing her child would behave? Is she deciding what to make for dinner? Is she worried about her children's future? Is she worried if her family is going to make it through this war? Does she lie in bed and pray for her family's safety? Does she get a knot in her stomach every time they announce another bomb has gone off?

I wasn't sure if I should put this one in the book. I was afraid some people would not understand why I put it in here, but decided if you are this far in the book and not offended. You won't be now.

*   *   *   *   *   *   *

The Other Side

In a small Iraqi village, Alihai walks through her door. Setting her abyss down by her market basket, she decides where to start. Her son is at her side still chattering away. She couldn't wait for him to start talking and now wonders if he will ever stop.

Later while cleaning dinner dishes she worries that her husband isn't home yet. Is he ok? Will there be a knock on her door? What would she do if something happened to him? This is all they have known. Before the war the worry was that he would say or do the wrong thing to the wrong person. He feels so strongly about their liberation, there was always that chance one of Saddam's henchmen would find out. Now that the Americans have come, they have a real chance at freedom. Yet he still puts his life in danger. He says he will help the Americans and if he dies in the process it is Allah's will.

Looking in on her children before going to bed, she leans on the doorway to watch them sleeping. Thinking they look like little angels. She worries about them being caught in a cross fire, or being too close when a bomb goes off. They are not dealing well with everything going on, but she doesn't know how to help them. As much as she wants the bloodshed to end, she wants freedom more. At least now there is hope.

*   *   *   *   *   *   *

Michael S. Hancock was killed on October 24, 2003, while guarding a grain plant. He was in C/ 1-320th of the 101st Airborne Division. He was very new to the battery, but already had left a huge impression. He had a wife and four precious children. There was a memorial service for him in Iraq and here at Ft. Campbell. What I've said about him tells you nothing about the person he was, but I didn't know him. I've been told he was a wonderful person. Even though I didn't know him, he has made a change in me. One I will not forget. I can honestly say that after his service and funeral, I will never again look at our flag the same. It was always important to me, but now I truly see everything it represents.

*   *   *   *   *   *   *

When A Soldier Dies

As I walk into the room, it's everything I can do to put one foot in front of the other. He looks so young. Seeing him in his class A's, he could be any of ours. As I walk away, I wonder will anyone truly appreciate his sacrifice?

I reach out to hug his wife, and give my meager words of comfort. She stands there so brave giving support to her children. I can't imagine how she is still standing. As I walk away, I wonder will anyone truly appreciate her sacrifice?

Looking around the service the other wives' eyes fill with tears. Their hearts break for this family. It also breaks for them, because in their mind they hear ' but for the grace of God there go I.' This hits too close to home and makes it all too real. I wonder will anyone truly appreciate their sacrifice?

As the casket rolls out into the hearse, his little boy says, " Bye Daddy, I love you." As I walk away, I wonder will anyone truly appreciate his sacrifice?

So the next time you hear a soldier has died, stop and think of the family he left behind. Think of them the next time you vote, speak your mind, or go to the church of your choice. Remember the little boy. I know I'll never forget him. Most of all truly appreciate the sacrifice this family gave to you for your freedom.

*   *   *   *   *   *   *

In today's paper it was published that there is a memorial trust fund for the children of Sgt. Hancock (he leaves behind 4 children ages: 3,7,9,10). Many of you have already asked about this, so I wanted you to get this information as soon as I knew something.

Memorial contributions may be made to:
Hancock Children Trust Fund
c/o Bank of America, Military Banking
Fort Campbell, KY 42223

*   *   *   *   *   *   *

The Wait

You come home after a fun day with friends. You've finally bought the plates to hang in the kitchen. It's so nice to have the occasional day where you can be light and fun.

You call your mother, so excited to hang your new plates. She asks if you had heard about the Black Hawks that went down in Mosul. Your heart drops. The new plates now forgotten. You hang up and check the news. As you remember your husband saying he had something to do today. Did that mean a mission or a run to the PX? It happened seven hours ago. How long before we find out who? Seventeen soldiers gone at once. You can't watch news but a minute, because the baby is still awake. You check the Internet, nothing new. No choice but wait and get on with life.

You go back to the plates. Now the interest is lost, but you need to be busy. Hours go by, you put the baby to bed. You check the news, nothing. No choice but wait and get on with life.

This time feels different. The feeling of dread won't leave. You never do this, but you feel you can't sleep if you don't ask. You call a friend that you know will hear things before you. She says try not to worry, he's okay. You know she knows who it is. The weight in your chest lifts. Now it's time to go to bed. No choice but wait and get on with life. So life doesn't get on without you.

*   *   *   *   *   *   *

On November 15, 2003, two Black Hawk helicopters went down. We lost seventeen soldiers at once, five of which were from C/ 1-320th of the 101st Airborne Division. This is the same battery that had just lost a soldier. All were from the same section. The papers don't talk about the injured and the fact their injuries were severe and life threatening. There were memorials here and in Iraq. I can't tell you how heartbreaking this was to see. This battery only had 56 soldiers in it and lost six plus two injured, all within two weeks, but they are soldiers so they drive on. I'll forever be amazed how much strength they have within them.

*   *   *   *   *   *   *

Dying Young

They were all so young. People say it's tragic, but at least they don't have kids. No, they don't have kids, they are kids. On one hand they were grown men who volunteered to go and fight for their country. These are not ordinary 18-22 year olds. These are heroes.

On the other hand, look around you, possibly in your own home at the young adults you know. Can you imagine them doing what these guys do everyday? Their life had yet to begin. They don't remember a world without TV remotes, VCR's, or microwaves.

It is such a tragic loss. If their short life were any indication of what the future would have brought, then we all have lost the great things they would have accomplished. It is sad the world will never get to see how destiny shaped them.

Why

I make my way through the crowd to find a seat. Looking at the seventeen wreaths in front of the stage, I just can't believe they are gone. I look around at the heavy hearts and sad eyes. As they play "American Soldier" I watch pictures roll across the large screen. I am struck with how many lives are affected by this loss. They don't just show them in uniform, but in life. One with his mom, another with his wife and son, and more with friends and family.

Tears surround me as we all try to comfort one another. Soldiers everywhere with more pain in their eyes than they will ever express. Looking as though they carry the weight of the world on their shoulders, but standing strong and tall as if they can carry it. You pray for everyone here and those still in Iraq to have the peace they need.

There are times in life when the questions don't have answers. This is one of those times. At times like this, you just have to believe that God is in control and He does have the answers.

Last Glance

The soldier leans against the back wall of the memorial service. Pain hangs in the air. He looks over the crowd so devastated by the loss of seventeen soldiers at once.

He watches as pictures of his friends in happier times roll across the screen. One at a time, people he knows get up to speak of the ones they loved. Knowing each one wishes they would have said these things while they had the chance. Now the words are for those left behind, as a tribute to these heroes.

The crowd is filled with everyone from privates to generals. So many wives here to show respect, while saying a silent prayer that their husband never has to be honored in this way. To his right and left soldiers line the walls. So many home from injuries. Each wondering had they been there, could they have done something to prevent the loss of so many? The misplaced responsibility will fade in time. One day soon they will realize some things are beyond their control.

He gazes over the sea of tears, finding his wife. Thinking to himself as he watches her. She is so lovely. I love her so much. She has been the joy of my life. She is so upset, her body trembling as she cries. Needing to give her some sort of comfort, I make my way to her. As I drift down the aisle people pass without recognition as though I'm not there. When I touch her shoulder she raises her eyes to me, and looks straight through me. Even though she can't see me I know she feels my presence. Her tears slow with a far away look in her eyes. I know she is remembering the feel of my arms around her, but my time has come to leave this world. I savor my last look at her until we meet at the gates of heaven.

* * * * * * *

I hate being one of those stereotypical women who know nothing about cars, but I am. I swear when my husband comes home, I'll take a class. I have had car repairs more months than not since he has been gone. The really hard part is you have to listen to mechanics advice because you have no way of knowing what is wrong. I am sure the same could be said of other things for other people, but cars are my weakness. I bet they could have made up an engine part and I wouldn't have known the difference. Maybe I'll go to trade school to be a mechanic. I could open a shop that only works on cars for women. That way they wouldn't have to worry about getting taken advantage of and they also could use "thingy" language without being looked at as if they were stupid. Now, I know there are lots of women that know about cars, I'm just not one of them.

* * * * * * *

While They Are Gone

Why is it that everything breaks, dies, or otherwise goes to hell in a hand basket while they are gone? You can putt along with no worries, until they leave. Then the car won't start, the toilet overflows, the roof leaks, and the bug guy says there are termites.

So you get a fix- it book, call friends and family for advice, and deal with it. Does "suck it up and drive on" ring any bells? Then your husband calls and asks is everything ok? You smile, nod, and say, "Don't worry about things here Honey, everything is fine. We just miss you." Instead of saying Murphy's Law is in effect, you need to come home and deal with these problems. At least come home long enough for me to have a break down, because I just don't have time right now.

So at the end of the day we can calculate batting averages, fix the leaky sink, change the car battery, and fix the table that broke in the move while he was deployed. The end result may not be perfect, but between 550 cord and 100 mile an hour tape we can handle anything.

One More Day

The phone rings. It is my girlfriend crying. What is wrong? What happened? " My husband", she tells me. My heart drops. Oh no, not her. She explains, " I was on the phone with him when sirens went off. I could hear them, they were so loud. He yells into the phone. ' I've got to go' and the line goes dead." I feel her fear through the phone. I ask, " How long ago?" " An hour," she replies. "Have you checked the news?" " No, because if I do I'll be on it all night." " Ok, I'll check for you." Nothing except Michael Jackson on the news, this is more important than what is happening with soldiers?

She spoke with her mother earlier; her mother says he is fine. She just wants to ease her daughter's worries, but the reality of it is she doesn't know if he is fine. For some reason, you can only get true comfort from another wife. The news announces a blast in Baghdad about thirty miles from her husband. My mind races for a reason. I say, " Maybe the sirens sounded to be prepared, just in case." It's a stretch, but with no other answers, this is the one to go with.

Much later her phone rings, it is him. There was fighting, but it's ok now. The fear passes and she marks one more day off the calendar.

*   *   *   *   *   *   *

Once we could meet on the Internet things improved by far. Wives and husbands alike were all set up on Instant Messenger. I would also have a few friends and their spouses on my messenger, so we could warn each other if one was running late. If a friend's spouse popped on, I could call my friend and let her know. It's a bad feeling to come home and realize you missed them.

We would agree on the next time we would meet or he would call. Knowing when helped in not keeping you so tied down. Unless, of course, he wasn't able to meet. Sometimes the computers were down, he would have something to do, or something would happen to a soldier and they would shut down access to computers. The more dependable your husband was to be there on time, the more it scared you when he wasn't. There was no way to know which reason it was.

*   *   *   *   *   *   *

10:00 am finds her in front of the computer waiting. 11:00 am comes and goes. She turns up the volume on the computer, so she can hear it through the house. Then gets on with whatever she needs to do. By 2:00 pm it starts to bug her. He is obviously not going to meet her. She does the time difference math and decides not to worry. She doesn't want to leave the house just in case he gets on. By 8:00 pm it bugs her bad. So she calls a friend to see if she has heard from her husband. She hasn't but was suppose to earlier today. She tells her friend not to worry; she is sure the computers are down and will be up soon. 9:00 pm " YAHOO" sounds through the house loud enough to wake the dead. She runs to the computer surprised he's on this time of day. No, not him. Another girlfriend curious to see if anyone has heard from the guys. She can now rule out her husband had something to do. She checks the news, no word of problems. She goes to bed.

The next day she is still waiting. Her mother comes to spend the night. So this keeps her pretty occupied. By that night she still hasn't heard from her husband. Since the wives' hot line is in full swing she knows no one else has either. She makes her mom's bed in the computer room, and goes to bed. 11:30 pm "YAHOO" screams through the house. Jumping straight out of bed she runs to the computer. Her poor mom thankfully not having a heart attack from the sudden noise, states " this is no way to live." Her husband explains that the computers were down, and he just got to a computer. He can't talk long just didn't want her to worry.

Once settled in bed she wonders what it must have been like for wives of previous wars? Was it better or worse not having information? While we have to deal with the day-to-day events of the war in our face, we have information and our generation has more contact with our soldiers than ever before. They had to wait months for a letter the whole time they were gone. Or worse back when notification was a list that came out in the paper or a telegram. She falls asleep with the thought that as frustrated as she gets, things are so much better than they use to be.

2nd Chance

After flipping another burger the smell of fresh cut grass hits him. A smell he missed. His wife walks out the back door to put more food on the table. She then comes over to hug him. As he puts his arms around her she says, "I just can't believe the change in you since you have been home. Lets not ever let things between us be like they were before you left." In a low loving voice he says, " Never again. I don't ever want to lose you and the kids."

His eyes pop open. It's dark; he knows he can't possibly be home, in the distance he hears muffled gunfire and the roar of attacking helicopters. Not home, Iraq. He leans up on his cot and reaches over to turn on the light. Picking up the letter from home to read once again, he glances over the room. Sand, sand, and more sand. It doesn't matter what you do it covers everything. After reading the letter he carefully folds it.

"Lord, please give me the time to make my dream a reality. If given the chance I will do it right this time."

Her eyes pop open. It's dark; she knows he can't possibly be home, she recognizes the sound of silence. Not home, Iraq. She leans up on her bed and reaches over to turn on the light. Picking up the letter from him to read once again, she glances over the room. The empty, lonesome bed stretches out before her. It doesn't matter how many pillows you add, it is still just as empty. After reading the letter she carefully folds it.

"Lord, please give me the time to make my dream a reality. If given the chance I will do it right this time."

*   *   *   *   *   *   *

One night I had heard two soldiers were killed in Mosul while driving. I went on the Internet to find more information. It would at least have been the next day before they released who was killed. I found some information about it and was shocked at the graphic details of what had happened to them. After, I was looking through general pictures of the war when I ran across close up pictures of those soldiers lying on the street. It was horrible. I immediately shut it off, but it was too late. The image will always be with me now.

*   *   *   *   *   *   *

*I want to make clear this is an exception to the rule. Most reporters, especially embedded reporters, are there risking their lives to get information back to us. They report responsibly, because they too are mourning their loss.

How can they report what they do, when they do? On one hand you want information as soon as it is available. On the other, is it too much to ask to keep the families of the deceased in mind? What kind of person puts detailed reports with horrible descriptions of the killing of soldiers on the news? Do they know notifications take time? It's automatic for families to look for information, only to stumble across pictures of the dead soldiers. Without knowing whose soldier he is. Do they know what families go through from the time they hear of deaths, to the time they know what soldier it is? What about their families? Do they realize the family doesn't need to live with that picture? Are they cruel or just insensitive? Do they know, or even care that there are wives all over Fort Campbell that will go to bed with that picture in their head? They will lie in bed willing sleep, wondering if it is their husband.

Reporters like you can say, " You are the ones surfing the channels for news. We are just providing it." They say " You want it, and then don't like it when you get it." That is the same as someone using honesty as an excuse for cruelty. That isn't just anyone lying there. That is an American soldier, a hero and no one has the right to treat him any differently. What you did was degrading to him and to responsible reporters risking their lives to get information back to us. Watch your step and show respect, because he died for your right to print this garbage.

*   *   *   *   *   *   *

I am so lucky that there are other men in my son's life that love him. While his father is gone he really needs the male attention.

It just makes me sad that he is making these memories with someone else. Someone else is teaching him how to fish, to ride a bike, and any number of other things.

I try to keep my husband informed of the changes in our son. He is so grateful that there are people there for his son, but it hurts he's not the one.

*   *   *   *   *   *   *

Pictures

The soldier walks in his tent shaking off the sand. As he collapses exhausted on his cot, he sees pictures of his family. He rolls on his back to stare at the tan ceiling, with the tan walls. He thinks to himself, God I miss them. It's been so long since I've held them. My son has grown from a toddler to a little boy while I've been gone. My wife, it's been so long since I've seen her lovely face. No matter how much I believe in fighting this war, it's hard leaving them. I feel such guilt not being there for my son and leaving everything on my wife's shoulders. She's strong and can handle anything. She has to be; she's a military wife. However, how much can one person be expected to take? I hear guys say they left babies and came home to kids that didn't recognize them. I believe in service to my country, but it is so hard to watch my son grow up in pictures. I pray I haven't become a voice on the phone or a picture on the wall. On the phone he says, " I miss you, Daddy. When are you coming home?" What do you say? What is the right answer? How do I say you are the most important thing in my life, and in the same breath say I don't know when I am coming home? I don't know the answers. I do know I will never again take for granted the picture I now carry in my mind of my sleeping wife and child snuggled in the bed beside me.

Rumors

Most of us who have been a military wife for very long know the pit falls. There are so many. One of the biggest is rumors. There is always someone watching, assuming things about you.

I know there are young wives that still want to go out and have fun. It may seem and be perfectly innocent. You and some girlfriends go to a club and if you dance it's with each other.

Seems innocent, right? Wrong. Some guy in Rear-detachment sees you and tells someone else, who tells his wife, who tells her friend, who tells her husband in Iraq. This soldier then goes to your husband. The story has changed so many times by this point, you wouldn't even know it's about you. This guy tells your husband you were seen in a bar with some guy. This couldn't be further from the truth, but your husband doesn't know that.

You say, "My husband trusts me. He would never believe anything like that." Keep in mind he has been gone a long time. He has also seen guys get Dear John letters and heard stories about other wives. Even if he dismisses it out right, that doesn't mean it won't nag at him. A lingering doubt in his mind. Even though this doesn't make sense, it is the way things go.

*   *   *   *   *   *   *

We all know kids take blame for things they can't possibly control. Also, we know they hear and see all. I think I messed up with my son. I sometimes forgot he could pick up on everything I felt. I did the best I could with him, but with hindsight I would do things very differently.

*   *   *   *   *   *   *

Momma says Daddy will be gone for a long time. She doesn't know when he will be home. Why doesn't she? Is he ever coming home?

Why doesn't he send a letter? I am waiting everyday when the postman comes. Momma says he will write when he can. Why doesn't he just put it in the mailbox? Is he ever coming home?

The older kids at school said soldiers get shot and die. My daddy is a soldier. Will he get shot and die? Is he ever coming home?

Why hasn't Daddy called? Momma always has a phone and always answers it. She says he will call as soon as he can. Why doesn't he just pick up a phone? Is he ever coming home?

I came in from outside and heard Momma talking to herself. She was fixing the toilet saying she was sick of doing everything herself. She was sick of being a single parent. She was sick of being alone. Does she not like being my parent? She's not alone, she has me. When I asked, she said she didn't mean it. She was just frustrated. Is he ever coming home?

Why doesn't Momma smile and laugh as much as she use to? She used to laugh when I did this, now she gets mad. Is it me? Am I just too bad? Is he ever coming home?

Why does Momma keep whispering and going outside to talk on the phone? At school today I heard about the soldiers that died. I guess she thinks it will make me sad if she tells me. Is he ever coming home?

Sometimes when Momma thinks I'm asleep I can hear her crying. There must be something very wrong. She says she just misses Daddy sometimes and crying makes her feel better. Is he ever coming home?

I overheard my grandparents saying that they didn't know how much more my momma could take. What is wrong with her? She is all I have, I can't lose her too. Is he ever coming home?

Momma says Daddy is a good soldier and knows what he is doing. We will just have to believe God will watch over him. I know God loves me, so I know He will bring my daddy home.

Of course, we all know God loves him no matter what happens. The scary part is he can rationalize it in his mind in this way and I would never know. He can take blame for things that I couldn't imagine. You can't address a problem if you don't know it exists. If we could only see in their hearts and minds, it would make our job so much easier.

Ordinary Man

He is just an ordinary man. You won't hear his name on television, in papers, or on the radio. He goes through life in his quiet way, doing all the things he should. He could be any man, but he's not.

He is a father. He shines with pride when he looks at his child. He struggles with decisions, so wanting to make the right one. He hurts to see his son stumble and not be able to do it for him, because he knows he has to teach him to be a man in this world.

He is a husband. He loves his wife and through his eyes she will always be young and beautiful. He is grateful for the years he has had with her, and looks forward to the years to come.

He is a soldier. He has calluses on his hands and feet from the long hard hours of work. He believes in what he does and serves his country with pride. He doesn't want to leave his family, but understands freedom doesn't come free. So when his country is threatened he will make the many sacrifices to defend her.

He isn't famous and doesn't have a lot of money, but he is rich in love and respect from everyone that knows him. He is what a man should be and what heroes are made of. The world would be a better place if this were the standard for ordinary.

Ladies
and
Gentlemen…
We got him!

The Day He Was Caught

This must be what it felt like for all the WWII wives when Germany surrendered. Saddam's capture to Iraqi freedom is what Hitler's capture would have been to WWII. You understand why the Iraqi people run out in the street to celebrate. You might even do it yourself if you didn't think the neighbors would commit you. Just the difference in people I guess. Can you imagine military wives pouring into the streets, dragging their kids, waving M-16's over their heads? The government would send a truckload of psychiatrists to us. They would think they had sent the guys on one too many deployments, and we have finally cracked.

Even though we don't rejoice in quite the same way. We all feel the relief, joy, pride, and sense of justice they do. I am so proud to be a military wife and do my part for my country. I know every American is grateful to have the military we have to defend us. It amazes me everyday what Americans can do when challenged.

Saddam

I saw a muted interview of him after his capture. He reached up to stroke his beard. How many men have I seen do this? It just seemed to strike me that he is just a man. We tend to make him larger than life, when this one person is so evil and he turns so many lives into nightmares. While we can't understand the evil, we have to acknowledge its existence. We in America can't even imagine the atrocities he inflicted on people everyday. Iraq has lived in hell for 35 years. This is what gave him the image of being invincible. Looking at him now shows him for what he is. He is just an old man vying for his life. He truly is no bigger or meaner than a schoolyard bully who picks on everyone. Until someone comes along, draws the line in the sand and stands up to him.

My Hero

It's not just one act that makes a man a hero. It's the way he lives his life day in and day out. It's the love and compassion he shows everyday, and the sacrifices he makes for those he cares about, and those unknown to him.

He's not a hero, because he will sleep in a tiny tent on the floor just to keep a promise to his son, or because he tries to live his life as an example to his son.

He's not a hero, because when my son wants a kiss in the mail, he writes, "When you feel the wind on your cheek that is God sending you my kiss."

He's not a hero, because he will always stand by those he loves, and does the right thing even when others don't.

He's not a hero, because he will do anything to protect his family's freedom, and when I see him in uniform my heart swells with pride.

He's not a hero, because when his country is threatened he will defend it no matter the sacrifices he makes.

He <u>is</u> a hero because he is all these things and more. His loyalty knows no bounds. He is everything a man should be. He is my husband, my lover, my best friend, my shelter in the storm, and yes, my hero.

Missed Call

Out for a day of shopping with a friend. Kids in school, housework is done. Life is as good as it gets with your husband gone.

The cell phone rings, and of course it's in the cart on the other side of the rack. It could be your husband; you never know when he'll be able to call. Since you never recognize your phone, who knows how long it has rung. You drop the clothes in your hands, and trips over your friend while diving in the direction of the sound.

Once at the cart, you realize the phone is at the bottom of the basket in your purse. Of course, it's at the bottom. Where else would it be when you need it? Shoving stuff around the basket you finally gets the phone. You press the button two seconds too late. You grit your teeth and grunt. Trying not to say out loud the words you are thinking. Calling the missed number, already knowing the answer. Yep, from a pre-paid calling card. Why did he call? He wasn't supposed to call today. Your mood has taken a turn for the worst.

The phone rings again. You answer without looking at the ID. You say "hello" so excited. Then you recognize your mother's voice. "Oh, it's you." Great, now you have hurt your mother's feelings. Just what you need. You soothe Mom's feelings and gets off the phone.

Well pooh; you've been looking forward to this shopping day and working to make sure you had everything done prior to it. You wonder did he call the house? Will he call back? You tell yourself there is nothing you can do about it now. Even though you know this, it's still hard to shake the funk. You might as well choose to be happy and enjoy the day. Being down won't go back in time and get you to the phone faster. You know, that pretty much sums up my outlook.

While it's sometimes hard to do, you have a choice. You can choose to let life's problems weigh you down and be miserable, or you can change what you can, turn the rest over to God, and choose to be happy.

* Side note- my mom was not happy about this one.

*　*　*　*　*　*　*

A girlfriend told me she would laugh until she has time to cry. Humor is a wonderful thing. My husband and I have had a running joke over the last 7 or 8 months about the various creatures he lives with in his room. As time goes by, it just keeps getting sillier. I even went as far as sending him a sympathy card. I sent him one for pets when he stepped on the scorpion he had given up on killing. When things are tough a little humor, no matter how silly, goes a long way.

*　*　*　*　*　*　*

The Pet

Once upon a time there was a scorpion named Abula Brusier. He and his little MRE- eating mouse friend, Omar, lived together. One day a soldier moved in their room. Then everything turned into mortal combat. Boots slammed down from above. Big metal bars came at you every time you went for food.

The soldier and I finally agreed on peace. I would stay out of his bed, if he wouldn't kill me. After agreeing to coexist, I believe the soldier came to think of me as a pet. Then one day my friend, Omar, ate one too many MRE's. The soldier took him out in the worst way, with a cap and some glue. This made me worry a little. Am I next? I decide to go on my nightly walks when he was gone. Thinking there's no need to tempt fate.

One night I headed out on my nighttime stroll and splat, a boot comes out of no where. No worries, my end was quick with pancake results. Then instead of just tossing me out the window, my soldier gave me a funeral. He wore his black P.T.'s, and even sang Amazing Grace as he flushed. Don't be sad. I'm sure I'll live on in the mind of my soldier as the pet that if you got too close to, will give you a gift that keeps on giving.

*   *   *   *   *   *   *   *

The holidays were harder than I thought. We have spent many holidays apart, but this time seemed different. I went home for Thanksgiving. I had Christmas here and at home. I did my best to make it happy and fun for my son, but it was forced. I just didn't have my heart into it.

*   *   *   *   *   *   *

Home For The Holidays

There is a huge spread of food arranged so prettily. Her family gathered around it. They go around the table from person to person, saying what they are thankful for this year. They are all thankful for very important things, but all she can think of is she's thankful her husband is alive and well in Iraq. She doesn't want to dampen the festive mood, but this is what she is truly thankful for this year.

While her family loves and worries about her husband they just can't understand. Even though we go on as though things are normal, they just aren't. There is always at least a little tension, so she can never truly let down. There is always a small part of her mind devoted to it no matter what she is doing.

How can you feel so lonely in a room full of people? This is her family, but she still feels like the odd man out. Seeing them with their families makes her miss him all the more. Being in the military, we are use to being apart on holidays. Christmas is hard and this year even more difficult. If she can just get through the holidays with the thought that hopefully next Christmas will find her at home with her husband and son.

Special Delivery From Iraq

A week before Christmas your child starts in, "Is it here yet?" You try to explain, "I told you Daddy's package will be here by Christmas Eve." He asks again the next day and everyday until Christmas Eve. Day after day he gets the same answer. "It won't be here until Christmas Eve."

Christmas Eve there's a knock on the door. My son so excited runs right into me trying to get to the door. I make a grab for him and miss him. He throws open the door, doing a dance around the box. " It's here! It's here!" he exclaims. Watching him open it you know all his other presents will pale in comparison. It could be a box of sticks and he would think it's gold. Only you know the most precious gift he got this past year from his dad was a snapshot of his dad holding a sign saying "Happy Birthday Boo Bear."

Watching your child run off to play with his new toy, you pick up the phone with a sigh. Your girlfriend answers the phone in an excited voice and tells you, "He opened that door so fast I thought I would break my neck getting off that porch." I explain, " I tried to stop him or at least slow him down. I just knew he was going to open the door and see you. I really appreciate it. It's getting harder and harder to pull it off. It means so much to him and it makes my husband not feel so left out."

One day I plan to explain just how special that one true gift his dad sent him was to us. The picture he sent was more precious than anything else he could have done.

Christmas Morning

I am the first to wake on Christmas morning, enjoying the quiet before the storm. The phone rings and I just know it is him. Taking the phone with me to let my husband wake up our son, I put it to his ear. Suddenly his eyes pop open, " Daddy it's Christmas!" With the phone attached to both of us, we run to see what Santa brought.

My son's eyes are shining. He is smiling from ear to ear as he announces, " See Momma, Santa didn't bring me a lump of coal!" Laughing for the first time that day, my husband stays on the line until our son is done unwrapping his gifts before saying goodbye. With just us on the line I ask, "Are you ok, Honey?" "I'm fine," he says. It breaks my heart to hear the sadness in his voice.

After hanging up, I stay alone in my room. I wonder who was putting on the bigger front, my husband or me? Neither wanting to upset the other. He has missed so much, this is just another in a long list of things missed. With a deep breath, I plaster a smile on my face and join the others to enjoy Christmas with my son and family.

*　　*　　*　　*　　*　　*　　*

I was indecisive on writing about my son's problems because they are such personal issues. I've decided I should share some, because he is by far not the only one. He started out with nightmares. You think you can shelter your kids from everything, but you cannot. They go to school and go out in public. He became a very angry little boy. He started getting in trouble at home and at school. Thank God, he has a wonderful school. Finding him a doctor was harder than one would think. They were full on post. Civilian doctors really didn't want to deal with him, because of his age. I went through several doctors. I finally called back on post and explained I needed help; they made room for my son and really helped him. He is doing so much better now. I wish I could go further into the problems he had, but that wouldn't be right to him.

*　　*　　*　　*　　*　　*　　*

The End Of The Rope

I am tired, just plain tired. I am tired of being a single parent, his arguing and his wall of attitude. He has been such an angry little boy. The doctor appointments. The feeling of helplessness, having no idea what you can do to help him. The hopelessness of knowing the one thing he needs, you can't give him. The frustration of having the school call yet again.

I am tired of making all the decisions on my own. It would be different if I weren't married, and my decisions only affected myself. Being unsure when I will next hear from my husband, I can't wait for him. I am used to handling things myself, even before the deployment. A year of it gets old. There are some things that come up that really need to be a joint decision.

I am tired of handling all the problems myself, money problems and things involving our child, issues with his family, issues with my family. A lot happens in a year's time.

I am tired of the worry, the unknown looming on the horizon. There is no way to truly know what is happening to them until they come home. He is on the other side of the world and everything is simply out of my control.

I am tired of the wait. Putting everything on hold until he comes home. Not knowing when that will be because with the military you just don't know what might change. Telling your child, be patient, it won't be much longer.

I am tired of putting on a brave face. It's been there so long it could crack at anytime. Telling people everything is ok, when it is not. You don't want to be a whiner, but you are just tired.

I am tired of coming up with answers I don't have. I don't know when he will call. I don't know when he will be home. I don't know if he received something, because I haven't spoken with him in two weeks. I don't know what to expect when he comes home. I just don't have the answers.

Most of all I am just tired of being alone. No one to lean on when I am weary. If a problem gets too hard, just having someone to talk it over with or help make a solution. A shoulder to cry on when the world gets too tough. The one person you can count on and tell him anything. He knows all your insecurities and doesn't give them a thought except to encourage you. The human touch, other than from your kids, you don't get that day-to-day contact. It's been a long year and I am ready to be done. One day soon I can close my eyes and this time when I open them he'll be there.

*   *   *   *   *   *   *

There is so much I want to do before my husband comes home. I'm just having trouble getting motivated. It is almost too good to be true. It seems like I've been waiting for so long. As if I believe it will go away, or something will change and I'll be setting myself up for heartbreak. When my husband gets to Kuwait I'll believe he is coming home. Then I'll be jumping out of my skin to get everything done and lose five more pounds. I believe I ate my way through this last year. Unfortunately, I'm not one of those women who get upset and can't eat. Then they lose weight and are smaller than ever. Oh no, I eat, and eat, and eat some more.

*   *   *   *   *   *   *

Tick Tock

They are so close to coming home, but close doesn't count. There are still soldiers dying. If we were holding our breath before, it doesn't compare to now. It's like walking on eggshells. We are gearing up for the homecoming here. They are packing and loading up there. They are still not home.

While they are just a few weeks away from being home, it just takes a moment to change everything. You feel so lucky to have made it through the war, the start of rebuilding, and the month of November. God knows I've thanked Him everyday for getting us through November. Everyday that passes is another day nothing has happened to him. How long can our luck hold out? You pray they don't get laxed because they are so close to leaving.

Even after they pack up, there is still the trip to Kuwait. There's no way to discreetly move that many people and that much equipment across the desert. The 101st has been such a high profiled division, you worry they may try to target them.

Our husbands are well trained and very good at what they do. It's not a lack of confidence in them that makes you worry. It's the things that are totally out of their control. It's hard to be prepared for someone who attacks like a coward. They know that they can't beat our guys, so they use underhanded means to take potshots at them. It's just as well we don't know exactly when they are leaving Mosul. It will be easier if we don't know they are making the trip until it is done, and we receive a call from Kuwait. Until then we will pray everyday and look toward the moment we can exhale.

As They Trickle In

Turning into your driveway, your son points out the window and yells, " My daddy has those bags." Looking across the street your eyes fill with tears. Your neighbor's husband is one of the first home. His A-bag sitting on the porch. His field jacket draped over it, with his kevlar on top. It sits there so perfect, as if a picture. Swallowing the tears, you agree with your son. " Yes, your daddy has those bags." He asks, " Does that mean my daddy is coming home?" "No son, we've discussed this over and over. Everybody's daddy does a different job, so they come home at different times. It won't be long now. He will be home soon."

On the way to the store, you see welcome home signs. With each passing day you see more and more. You understand their excitement. You'll be the same way when yours comes home. Wishing he didn't have the MOS he does, won't change anything. No matter how sad it makes me that it's not mine, I am so glad they have their husband. It won't be long now. He'll be home soon.

Taking out the trash, the familiar scent of a grilled steak hits you. You feel very alone. It's not the steak; it's the man who used to cook it. It's snuggling up to him, smelling the charcoal. It's watching him play with the kids as he cooks. It's your family sitting around the table laughing. It won't be long now. He'll be home soon.

Standing in Wal-Mart convinced you have finally lost your mind, as you tear up looking at pre-made cakes. It's all you can do not to cry looking at one in particular. It has an eagle with a flag in the background, and across the top and bottom reads Welcome Home Daddy. It's won't be long now. He'll be home soon.

My son coming home from school sad and withdrawn. "Honey, what is wrong?" He says, "Bobby's dad came home. I want my daddy." As I pull him in my lap for a hug, I tell him, " I know, I do too. It won't be long now. He will be home soon."

My girlfriend dropping her daughter off on the way to the hanger. Even at 4:00 am, her eyes glowing and her face shining from the joy within her. Later, when she calls to check on her daughter there is no mistaking the excitement in the background. I hang up the phone with a sigh. Telling myself over and over it won't be long now. He will be home soon.

He calls and tells me, "you won't hear from me again until I arrive in Kuwait." Unsure exactly when they will start the trip I avoid the news. After the first day, I received word they had left Mosul and are headed south. I started cleaning the office.

Flipping through the channels, I catch a news flash of an attack on a convoy in Iraq. I realize his isn't the only convoy there, but it still makes me nervous. Waiting for more information, I'm stuck on the news. Great, you would think after a year of this I would know to turn off the news and walk away. I start cleaning the kitchen.

Later I received another e-mail, they have gone through the Sunni triangle and all is well. Thank goodness, I was worried about the trip and especially through the triangle. I'll breathe a little easier when they arrive in Kuwait, but I won't truly breathe until he is home. I start cleaning the closets.

The next day I received word they had arrived safely in Kuwait. Tears of relief fill my eyes, as I read the e-mail to a friend. Whether I'm crazy or just relieved doesn't matter. All that matters is he is finally out of Iraq. The weight in my chest is easing. I'm starting on the garage.

Two days later I hear from my husband. Finally, I can believe he is coming home. Reality sets in on me. That means I had better get real busy, real fast, and get a lot done in a short amount of time. At least it will keep me from watching the clock. At times like this, days can feel like weeks.

72 hours out she receives a phone call, he is on his way. Thrilled, she has to bite her tongue not to tell her child, she knows better. Everything is always subject to change. She immediately starts on the house.

48 hours later she receives another call, the plane has been delayed. " We will call as soon as we get information." By this point her son knows something is going on, because she has cleaned out the same closet three times. Still, she won't say anything to him.

16 hours later she receives yet another call. They are landing in eight hours, be at the parade field two hours early. Six hours: at this point she decides to tell her son. They both hurry to get everything ready.

Arriving at the parade field, she boards the bus with the other wives. By the time she gets to the hanger, her son is so excited he is all but climbing up her leg. Waiting, waiting. She is nervous and excited all at once.

Finally they come through the back door. She already knows he has to go through formation and a speaker before she can go to him. It's just the way it is. Her four year old doesn't take the news as well. She promises him everything in the world, if he will just wait until we are allowed to go to Daddy. She understands, it takes all her restraint not to run to him. She wonders if the speaker is making an effort to speak slowly.

Finally she can go to him. Trying to remind herself it will only be for twenty or thirty minutes and then they will leave for three more hours. It's hard, but she knows if it weren't done this way she wouldn't be able to have even thirty minutes. They will always have to be soldiers first. They have no choice; they have a country to defend.

First Sight

Waiting in the hanger, waiting, waiting. I can't stand another minute. I can barely contain my excitement. I've envisioned his homecoming so many times, for so many months, all smiles and laughter.

Finally, here they come. Where is he? He breaks from the crowd. Oh God, it has been so long since I've seen his handsome face. As I run to him I falter. Suddenly I stop, my face in my hands, overcome with pent up emotion. I've held so much in under the brave face I show to everyone. The relief that he is finally home safe, alive, and soon in my arms. I can't seem to move forward. Then suddenly I feel strong arms around me holding me up. Leaning into him as I've wanted to do for so long. Thank God, it's over. As he lifts our son and hugs us both, I say a quick prayer. Thank you, Lord, for bringing him home to me.

Even though, I know he's only home until the next time he is called to serve. I won't give thought to it. I can only be happy and thankful for the here and now. I'll enjoy every minute I have with him.

Coming Home

I'm finally home, what now? Where do I fit in my family? What is my place? She does and handles everything. She's had to; there was no one else. Where am I needed? She is so independent. I knew she could handle it, and I am so very proud of her. I just want to find my place. I want to help, but where do I start. She has her own rhythm and routine. What is helping, what is not?

My son naturally looks only to her, because she is all he has had. I don't want to change what is obviously working. I just want to find my place. It was so easy when I left, why is it so awkward now? Should I ask her or just act as though nothing is wrong? Will that make it worse or better? I guess I thought I would find them the way I left them. I left and in my mind time stopped. I love them both so much. I'll just have to be patient. Give all of us time, and my place will come to me.

Dear God,

Thank you so much for bringing my husband home to me safe and sound. Please keep watch over the ones still there, and give their families the strength they need to endure. Please give the families of those we lost the peace that they need to start rebuilding their life. Be with the returning soldiers and ease the burden of their war memories. Help heal the wounds of the injured soldiers. Help the Iraqi people make the right decisions for their country. Keep the evil men out who want to create terror. Allow Iraqi children to grow up as friends of America. Please don't let it slide back into the horror that it was, and then all of this would have been for nothing. Please guide our leaders in the war on terror; they need You now more than ever. Help me teach my little boy that every time my husband goes out the door doesn't mean it will be for a year. Dear Lord, please give me the wisdom I need to help my family heal from the separation and rejoice in the reunion.

Your faithful servant,

Sherry

*   *   *   *   *   *   *

I thought the cover was so perfect for the book. It is a postcard made in 1919. My great-grandfather brought it back from WWI. I wanted to use it for many reasons, one of which was the feelings it expresses of war that we still feel today. We are not just connected to each other but to the families of wars past. Families from the Revolutionary War to present day have done their part from sending letters, prayers and keeping the home front going, to fighting in the war themselves. We come from a tradition of amazing people. While times and circumstances change, we all know the heart break of war.

*   *   *   *   *   *   *

*　*　*　*　*　*　*

My great- grandfather, Willie Travis, was in WWI. He was a farmer, and had lived in rural Tennessee all his life. Country life tended to be very basic. There were things he knew a lot about, but he wasn't worldly. When your main goal everyday is to ensure food is on your table, your world and knowledge is centered on what makes that happen. We live in the information age with instant news. So we can't imagine someone being unaware of what is going on in the world.

When I was about ten years old I was studying WWI in school. I asked Daddy Travis if he was in WWI. He said, " Yes, I fought in the war." I asked, "What was it about?" He said, "I didn't know. I was in France and I fought in the war." His country needed him and he went. That was all he knew. Even at ten, I was floored that he fought in a war and didn't even understand it. Why would he be willing to fight in a war he knew nothing about?

I'm not saying his way is how things should be. This is our country and we the people were meant to run it. The people in Washington are there to represent us. However, it will amaze me all my life that all he needed to know was that his country needed him and he was there.

*　*　*　*　*　*　*

Do you ever feel like you want to do something to help, but don't know what you can do? On the next few pages I have suggestions, or you can call your nearest military post and they can tell you how you can help. Thank you ahead of time for anything you might do, it is so appreciated.

Injured troops are arriving at **Walter Reed Army Medical Center**, Washington, DC without suitable clothing for a hospital stay. The fabulous medical service personnel on the battlefield in Iraq and Afghanistan are doing such a tremendous job of keeping many of our troops alive after they are wounded, they (hospital) are having more injured than expected.

The service members need:

- pajamas (top & bottoms)
- Sweat pants/sweatshirts
- Tee shirts
- Or anything that one can wear with a leg or arm cast or heavy dressing on a wound
- They would also love to have paper, envelopes and stamps

The address is Any American Soldier, Sailor, Airman or Marine, Walter Reed Army Medical Center, 6900 Georgia Avenue North West, Washington, DC 20307.In bottom right front write "clothing".

The USO www.uso.org

CONTINGENCY TRAVEL FUND

Traveling is a challenge in the first place. But when a family is rushed away from home following the devastating news that their loved one has become a war casualty, travel details become low-priority. These details, however, do not take care of themselves. Facing the daunting task of identifying the remains of their loved one in a strange place, these families need someone to reach out to them and offer support. The USO is there, ready with emergency funds for families in need. These funds will be used for food, hotel expenses, airfare, etc. This is a need that will only increase with intensity until Operation Iraqi Freedom has come to completion. Won't your corporation consider funding this critical project?

USOCARES.ORG

The USO is enlisting individuals around the world to support the troops through Care Package. These packages are being delivered to armed forces deployed around the world to show them they are not forgotten. With a $25 donation you can sponsor a care package personal message of support and encouragement. Corporations interested please contact questions@usocarepackage.org www.operationuplink.org

Until they come home,
We'll bring them voices from home.

Operation Uplink is a unique program that keeps military personnel and hospitalized veterans in touch with their families and loved ones by providing them with a free phone card. Using contributions from supporters like you,

Operation Uplink purchases phone cards and distributes them to servicemen and women who are separated from those they care about.

Since the events of Sept.11, 2001, the need for operation uplink phone cards has risen dramatically.

For more information, contact Linda Ferguson at 816-756-3390.

About Operation Hero Miles

Operation Hero Miles provides a way for you to help our troops stationed in Iraq and Afghanistan by donating your unused frequent flyer miles. Efforts are underway to make the donated miles more broadly available to all U.S. military personnel.

The Hero Miles Story:

In September 2003, the Pentagon started giving soldiers stationed in Iraq two-week leaves in the largest R & R program since the Vietnam War. Soldiers on R & R or Emergency Leave are flown by the military to Germany or three airports in the United States, Baltimore/Washington, (BWI), Dallas/Fort Worth, (DFW), or Atlanta, (ATL) for free.

Existing law in 2003 required soldiers to pay for their own flights home from these three airports. The Hero Miles program was started to provide free round trip tickets donated by the American public to the almost 500 soldiers arriving each day from Iraq on **R & R Leave** last fall. This public response helped persuade Congress to change the law and beginning January 1, 2004, the Pentagon now pays for these domestic flights for the soldiers.

Not long after the Hero Miles program started, the U.S. Army contacted the Congressmen and requested that donated tickets also be made available to soldiers who must return home on **Emergency Leave**. These soldiers are approved to return home by their Commanders to attend to the birth, death, or illness of a family member or other family emergencies. Even today the military does not pay for any domestic travel for these soldiers or their families once the soldier arrives in the U.S. and their military base. For example, a soldier might be returned from Kirkuk, Iraq to his U.S. departure station at Fort Hood, Texas to attend to the funeral of his mother-in-law in Pennsylvania. However, he must personally pay the cost to travel to Pennsylvania for himself and his wife and children who are stationed at Fort Carson, Colorado at his permanent duty station. Your donation of frequent flyer miles can help the military provide free transportation for families in this situation.

In December 2003, senior Pentagon officials met with Congressman Ruppersberger and proposed a further expansion of the Hero Miles program. In partnership with the Fisher House Foundation (locations), Hero Miles tickets are now used to fly **family members of wounded soldiers** to U.S. military hospitals and be at the bedside of their loved ones. Often these families have to make many trips and stay for months at a time to help seriously wounded soldiers through long recuperations and multiple surgeries. The Fisher House provides free lodging for the families and Hero Miles provides transportation.

Americans have donated their unused frequent flyer miles to the Department of Defense and the Fisher House Foundation to help troops travel home and spend quality time with their loved ones, without worrying about how much it will cost. Airlines currently taking donations are Northwest, Pan-Am, and Southwest.

www.taps.org

The Tragedy Assistance Program for Survivors, Inc. (TAPS) provides a wide variety of programs and information to survivors, military and casualty personnel and others. TAPS is a national non-profit organization made up of, and providing services to, all those who have lost a loved one while serving in the Armed Forces. The heart of TAPS is our national military survivor peer support network. They also offer grief-counseling referral, caseworker assistance and crisis information, all available to help families and survivors cope and recover.

They provide these services 24 hours a day free of charge! Please call us at 1-800-959-TAPS (8277) or e-mail us at info@taps.org if we can help.

T*A*P*S is currently "gearing up" for this year's 29th Annual Marine Corps Marathon, which will take place Sunday, October 31, 2004 in Washington, D.C. T*A*P*S would like to invite everyone to a part of TEAM T*A*P*S in one way or another. Please come be apart of this wonderful race filled with much patriotism and camaraderie. The following are some of the special ways you can become a member of TEAM T*A*P*S.

You can be a:

1. **Runner**
2. Host a survivor
3. TAPS supporter
4. mcm volunteer on behalf of team TAPS

5. virtual runner

****

www.commissaries.com

Commissary Gift Certificates can be purchased several ways

- **Purchase to give as a gift to an authorized shopper** for a special occasion. Go to "Designate your Gift of Groceries."
- **Purchase and take delivery**, then forward to a military relief organization locally. Go to "Designate your Gift of Groceries."
- **Elect to donate through one of three non-profit organizations:** the Air Force Aid Society for military families worldwide, the USO (for service members overseas), or Fisher House Foundation for families staying in one of 30 comfort homes near military hospitals worldwide. Once there are enough donated certificates to pass along, CertifiChecks bundles them up and forwards them to the designated charity which then distributes them as the need arises.

****

The Fisher House program is a unique private-public partnership that supports America's military in their time of need. The program recognizes the special sacrifices of our men and women in uniform and the

hardships of military service by meeting a humanitarian need beyond what normally is provided by the Department of Defense. These homes enable family members to be close to a loved one at the most stressful time -- during the hospitalization for an unexpected illness, disease, or injury.

There are currently 32 houses located on the grounds of every major military medical center and several VA medical centers. These houses play a key role and are a vital asset to our military by allowing them to care for casualties, and their families.

It is our goal to create *"a home away from home"* that allows guest families the opportunity to address any challenge they must face during a time of crisis with dignity, and to give them a sense that there really are those who care about them in their time of need.

HOW YOU CAN GET INVOLVED

Please note: At Fisher House it is our policy that 100% of funds designated for a specific purpose are to be used for that purpose. We do not charge a percentage against your donation to cover overhead. Nor do we pay any processing fee on your credit card donation. At Fisher House our overhead percentage from our last audit was 7.1 %.

You have many opportunities to get involved and bless these families in need:

HELP SPONSOR A FAMILY

Your gift will be used to help meet the cost of lodging for a family whose loved one was injured in Operation Enduring Freedom or Operation Iraqi Freedom. There is a limit to the number of families who can stay in a Fisher House. We are committed to help provide lodging for families who must find commercial lodging, because the Fisher House is full.

HELP PROVIDE FOR BASIC NEEDS

Fisher House supports military personnel wounded in action and those seriously ill being treated in military hospitals in the U.S. and overseas. Your donation of "Gifts from the Homefront" certificates will ease the burden for military personnel and their families at a most stressful time in their lives.

HELP PROVIDE FOOD AND STAPLES

Fisher House is proud to be one of a select group of national organizations participating in a special program that provides military families in need with gift certificates that can be used to buy food and staples through the commissary (the military's grocery store). Your gift can help meet the basic needs of a family during a stressful time.

SEND A MESSAGE TO OUR WOUNDED HEROES

You can send a note of encouragement and gratitude that can be read by a service member who has been wounded or injured in Operation Iraqi Freedom or Enduring Freedom.

HONORING THEIR SACRIFICE

You can help support a soldier's spouse and children whose parent has given their life in defense of our country. We are establishing a fund to express our gratitude and provide assistance for the family left behind to help meet their needs until military benefits can begin.

We will soon have our own Fisher House at Ft. Campbell

****

www.saluteheros.org - A wonderful web site, I would like everyone to go check it out.

- **Corporate Sponsorships** provide a way for your business -- large or small -- to make a direct impact on how we can assist our heroes
- **Volunteer To Help** in your local community.
- **Make A Donation** None of our programs to benefit our heroes can exist without your support. Please help today.
- **Tell Us How Your Organization Can Help:** Volunteer your civic organization, professional group, or

hobbyist club and tell us how you can help SAH in your own unique way.

We will help our heroes by launching the following programs:

- The First Annual Road to Recovery Conference and Tribute at Walt Disney World in December 2004

- Homes for Paralyzed Heroes project which will build and modify homes for those heroes who are wheelchair bound

- Family Support Network to provide travel and lodging assistance for families visiting wounded relatives in hospitals

- Hire A Hero program to help find jobs for wounded veterans

All of the charities are wonderful, but this one is near and dear to my heart. These are soldiers helping soldiers. I am so proud of them. After everything they have been through, they have the courage to put their self out there in the public eye to help others. I hope all of you do whatever you can for the organization.

Printed in the United States
73580LV00002B/7